Debra Oswald is a writer for stage, film, television and children's fiction.

Her stage plays have been produced around Australia. *Gary's House*, *Sweet Road* and *The Peach Season* were all shortlisted for the NSW Premier's Award. Her play *Dags* has had many Australian productions and has been published and performed in Britain and the United States. *Gary's House* has been on the senior high school syllabus, and has been performed in translation in both Denmark and Japan. *The Peach Season* won the 2005 Seaborn Playwright's Prize. *Mr Bailey's Minder* broke the Griffin Theatre's box office record in 2004, toured nationally in 2006, and was produced in Philadelphia in 2008.

Debra has written two plays for **atyp** (Australian Theatre for Young People). *Skate* was performed in Sydney, on a NSW country tour and at the Belfast Theatre Festival. *Stories in the Dark* premiered at Riverside Theatre Parramatta in 2007. *House on Fire* premiered at **atyp** in 2010.

She is the author of three 'Aussie Bite' books for kids, including *Nathan and the Ice Rockets*, and five novels for teenage readers: *Me and Barry Terrific*, *The Return of the Baked Bean*, *The Fifth Quest*, *The Redback Leftovers* and *Getting Air*.

Among Debra's television credits are 'Bananas in Pyjamas', 'Sweet and Sour', 'Palace of Dreams', 'The Secret Life of Us' and award-winning episodes of 'Police Rescue'. She is the writer and creator of the multi-award-winning series 'Offspring'.

Darcie Irwin-Simpson (left) as Bec and Claudia Brooks as Charlotte in the 2010 **atyp** *production in Sydney.*
(Photo: Alex Vaughan)

HOUSE ON FIRE

DEBRA OSWALD

CURRENCY PRESS
SYDNEY

CURRENCY TEENAGE SERIES

First published in 2011
by Currency Press Pty Ltd,
PO Box 2287, Strawberry Hills, NSW, 2012, Australia.
enquiries@currency.com.au
www.currency.com.au

Reprinted 2014

NATIONAL LIBRARY OF AUSTRALIA CIP DATA

Author: Oswald, Debra.
Title: House on fire / Debra Oswald
ISBN: 9780868198880 (pbk.)
Target Audience: For secondary school age.
Subject: Sisters—drama.
Dewey Number: A822.3

Typeset for Currency Press by Dean Nottle.
Cover image: (front) Darcie Irwin-Simpson as Bec, Xenia Goodwin as
Michaela and Stephanie Jaja as Evie; and (back) Nathalie Fenwick as India in
the 2010 **atyp** production (Photo: Alex Vaughan).
Cover design by Emma Vine, Currency Press.

Contents

Currency Press acknowledges the Traditional Owners of the Country on which we live and work. We pay our respects to all Aboriginal and Torres Strait Islander Elders, past and present.

*Darcie Irwin-Simpson as Bec in the 2010 **atyp** production in Sydney. (Photo: Alex Vaughan)*

An Interview with the Author

atyp: *How did you come to playwriting?*

DO: I wrote stories all through primary school. But once I started going to the theatre when I was eleven, I was intoxicated by the idea of writing for the stage. I read every play I could find in the library, bashed out plays on my typewriter and posted them off to theatre companies in big padded envelopes. Luckily for me, I started writing so young, I was too naïve to be self-conscious or afraid of rejection. It's different now!

atyp: *What do you like best about theatre?*

DO: I like the special connection between live actors and a live audience. When it works, I love the sense of ritual with a play: everyone being together in a room to watch a story happen.

atyp: *Who are your biggest influences as a writer?*

DO: I enjoy lots of different kinds of writing. Early on, I was influenced by the writers I had the chance to see and read—people like Arthur Miller, Chekhov, Dorothy Hewett, Tennessee Williams, Joe Orton and others. One of my favourite plays more recently is *Angels In America*. These days I'm probably more influenced by novels I read and by good TV writers, for example David E. Kelley ('Boston Legal'), Tina Fey ('30 Rock') and Paul Abbott ('Shameless').

atyp: *What was your inspiration for* House on Fire*?*

DO: *House on Fire* came about because a girls' school (SCEGGS) asked me to write a play to be performed by an ensemble of drama students. I did some sessions with students where we explored the things in their lives that excited them, troubled them, made them laugh or agonise.

My job then was to write a play with lots of young female roles and with a story which would hopefully grab a teenage audience.

atyp: *What do you want the audience's experience to be while watching the play?*

DO: I want an audience to be swept away into the world of the story. I want people to laugh, feel moved and be surprised. I hope audiences will care about the characters and have some of their assumptions and judgements about people challenged.

For an audience of young people in particular, I hope the play will ring true. Even though the style of *House On Fire* is over-the-top, I hope there is an underlying honesty about how things work and how they feel for teenagers.

The play is about that moment that happens somewhere in your teens or soon after, when it suddenly strikes you that you're facing the world on your own. The years of feeling looked-after are over and you have to handle whatever life throws at you. A lot of young people feel anxious about the future, afraid of bombing out, madly trying to find a system that makes sense.

The Conway sisters in *House On Fire* face challenges that may be more tragic and more ridiculous than most of us, but I hope their story will resonate with lots of people.

The play is about the random forces in the world—you can't control them but you can withstand them better with the support of human connection.

atyp: *How do you feel about your work travelling from the page to the stage?*

DO: I don't think I'll ever lose the thrill of seeing a play go from the page to the stage. I still feel a childish excitement that all these clever people are helping my play come to life. Hearing the first read-through with the cast is always wonderful and teaches you a lot about your own play—what's working, what isn't, what needs to be cut.

I am always in awe of design, lighting and sound people who can see and hear things I can't and who will make my play seem better.

I've seen different productions of many of plays and it's fascinating to observe the different approaches people have taken to the material.

And then there's the moment the play gets in front of an audience—ah, that's both terrifying and exhilarating.

atyp *produced* House on Fire *in 2010*

Acknowledgements

Debra Oswald would like to thank Inga Scarlett, Jo Turner, SCEGGS, Richard Glover, Michael Wynne, and everyone from the SCEGGS and the **atyp** productions.

House on Fire was developed with the assistance of SCEGGS Darlinghurst.

Australian Government

Australia Council
for the Arts

Publication of this title was assisted by the Commonwealth Government through the Australia Council, its arts funding and advisory body.

First Production

House on Fire was commissioned and first produced by SCEGGS Darlinghurst at the Parade Playhouse, NIDA, Sydney, on 10 June 2009, with the following cast:

India	Airlie Dodds
Evie	Natasha Bassett-Tingey
Michaela	Laura Hopkinson
Bec	Claudia Osborne
Petra	Finola Sulman
Charlotte	Rosie Connolly
Kristin	Jemima Single
Alice	Kate Chalmers
Anna	Leila Enright
Researcher	Isabella Wood
Natalie	Adriana Notaras

Director, Ms Inga Scarlett
Assistant Director, Ella Parkes-Talbot
Production Associate, Kate Fisher
Set Designer, Simon Greer
Lighting Designer, Roger Hind
Technical Adviser, Eddi Goodfellow

House on Fire was subsequently produced by **atyp** at Studio 1, The Wharf, Sydney, on 3 June 2010, with the following cast:

Charlotte	Claudia Brooks
Petra	Ines English
India	Nathalie Fenwick
Natalie	Shenoa Fox
Alice	Lucy Freyer
Michaela	Xenia Goodwin
Bec	Darcie Irwin-Simpson
Evie	Stephanie Jaja
Researcher	Belal (Billie) Mansour
Kristin / Mia	Amy Mitchell
Security Guard	Patrick Richards

Director, Jo Turner
Assistant Director, Ashley Richardson
Designer, William Bobby Stewart
Lighting Designer, Verity Hampson
Sound Designer, James Brown

Characters

India, 12, super-intelligent, socially awkward

Evie Conway, 15, confused, unconfident but lively

Michaela Conway, 17, high-achiever, perfectionist, prone to guilt, takes care of everyone

Bec Conway, 20, prickly, clever, sarcastic, fiercely protective of her sisters; the burnout sister

Charlotte, 15, manipulative, pretty, charismatic

Alice, 15, Charlotte's giggly satellite

Kristin, 15, Charlotte's hard-faced henchwoman

Store Security Person, early 20s

Researcher, early 20s

Petra, 17 or 18, Michaela's friend, earnest, passionate vegan

Natalie, 17 or 18, Michaela's friend

Casting Note

The play has 11 roles that can be performed by female actors. With doubling of roles it is possible to have a smaller cast.

Several roles can become male roles: the Researcher, the Store Security Person, India (becoming Indio), Petra (becoming Peter). To switch gender on those roles, a few personal pronouns and words can be changed to suit.

Scene One

Prologue.
INDIA appears on stage. She's about twelve, wired-up, sharp-eyed.
INDIA is awkward with other characters but enjoys her role as narrator with puckish glee.

India [*addressing the audience*] I'm going to tell you the story of how the house next door to me burnt down. Did you know that in the United States alone, someone dies in a fire every one hundred and sixty-two minutes? Oh, don't worry—no-one is going to die in this fire. It's not that kind of story. I've lived next door to the three Conway sisters since I was a little kid. Evie Conway's fifteen.

> *EVIE appears in a spotlight, wearing an ugly bridesmaid dress. She talks on her mobile.*

Evie Hi, Charlotte. No, I'm still stuck at the wedding reception. They made me be a bridesmaid. Oh my God, the dress is so hideous I cannot tell you. It's made of this stiff sticky-outy material and the colour is totally barfable. Hey hey, I'll send you a photo!

> *EVIE holds her mobile out to take a photo of herself in the dress.*

India Evie was a bridesmaid because this was the weekend her father got married.

Evie [*on the phone to CHARLOTTE*] The woman he married? Get this: she was the Geography teacher at my old school. It's beyond embarrassing. I wasn't going to tell a single person but now I've blabbed to you so that shows I can't control my big mouth! You won't tell anyone, will you? Anyway anyway, what are you doing this weekend?

> *EVIE exits, yapping on her phone.*

India Evie's older sister Michaela is seventeen.

> *MICHAELA appears in a spotlight. She's wearing an identical bridesmaid dress.*

She's an academic high-achiever, school captain, coach of the junior netball team, leader of a Youth Against Poverty fundraising drive and a very nice person.

She waves and smiles hello to someone offstage, super polite.

Michaela Hello, Mr Davis. Mmm, it was a lovely wedding. Oh yes, I'm studying hard for the exams.

India The wedding happened on the weekend just before the start of the HSC exams.

MICHAELA switches on an mp3 player and chants study facts as she listens.

Michaela Born Gaius Octavius, 63 BC. Caesar assassinated, 44 BC. War with Sextus Pompey, 38 BC. 38 BC. 38 BC.

MICHAELA pauses the mp3 player and takes some calming deep breaths. She's under a lot of pressure. She exits, chanting Ancient History dates to herself.

India The oldest sister is Bec. She moved out of the house last year.

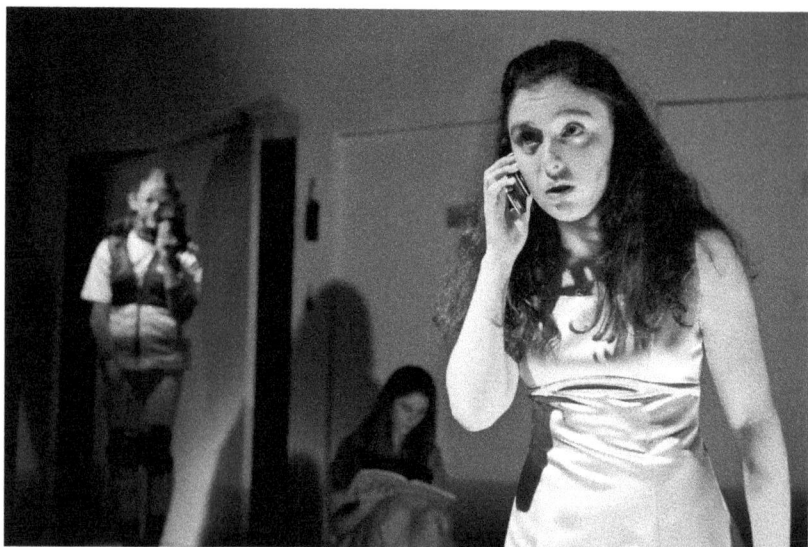

*From left: Nathalie Fenwick as India, Xenia Goodwin as Michaela and Stephanie Jaja (foreground) as Evie in the 2010 **atyp** production in Sydney. (Photo: Alex Vaughan)*

Spotlight on BEC, slouching, hair matted from sleeping, wearing pyjama pants and a singlet, eating uncooked two-minute noodles. Nearby, there's a third identical bridesmaid dress on a hanger, still in its plastic cover.

She moved out because—well, I used to hear heaps of loud arguments between Bec and—

Bec [*to the audience, indicating INDIA*] This kid next door—India—she's one weird little girl.

India [*to BEC*] Sorry? What are you doing? I'm the narrator!

Bec [*to INDIA*] Well, I guess you're not the only narrator.

India But you can't just start blabbing to the audience when I'm already—

Bec [*to the audience*] She's only twelve but she's *gifted*, mega IQ and all that. She's home-schooled and so bored the little brainiac spends half the day stickybeaking on neighbours. She's always—

INDIA retaliates by offering the audience juicy dirt on BEC.

India Bec dropped out of Law at uni. Now she lives in a rathole and her life's a mess.

BEC smiles and bows.

Bec I'm the burnout sister.

BEC goes back to eating the noodles.
We hear the beep of an answer machine and then recorded voices.

Manageress [*a voice on the machine*] This is a message for Bec Conway. Because of the economic downturn, we've had to lay off all casual bar staff. All your shifts are cancelled. So, uh—yeah—sorry.

Bec Which means I'm unemployed again. I also got a message from my flatmate.

Flatmate [*a voice on the machine*] I talked to the guy and he said we're evicted, like, for sure.

Bec Demolition guys turn up on Monday to knock this place down which is about as evicted as you can get.

BEC sighs deeply and ambles off.
INDIA is relieved to go on with the story alone.

India So this weekend Bec, Michaela and Evie's father got married. Afterwards the dad and his new wife flew away on their honeymoon. Vanuatu.

We see MICHAELA, now dressed in normal clothes. She's waving them off.

Michaela Have a great time, Dad. No really, don't feel guilty. The HSC's not as much of a big deal as people make out. You don't need to hang around and hold my hand.

India [*to the audience*] I told you she was a really nice person.

Michaela [*to her dad*] And don't worry. I'll take care of the house and look after Evie. You have fun!

India So that left Evie, Michaela and Bec Conway on their own.

We see all three sisters in separate spotlights.

The other information I should tell you is what happened a year and a half ago.

The sisters all stare ahead, overwhelmed.

Bec, **Michaela** & **Evie** [*together*] Mum…

India A man driving along the freeway had a heart attack.

There could be sound effects of a car accident or a violent burst of music. Maybe car headlights or some kind of disorienting lighting effect.

Bec His truck veered across to the wrong side of the road.

India And collided with the car being driven by Mrs Conway.

Bec It was a freak accident.

India No-one's fault.

Each of the three sisters is separately channelling her feelings in her own way.

BEC plays loud music on headphones, jerking her body to the beat, possibly singing harshly along with the music. We could hear the angry thumping music she is playing.

MICHAELA clutches at a book or a diary, wired-up, searching through the pages as if answers will be there.

EVIE is curled up, crying, like a little kid.

4

When her mum died, Michaela was in Nepal building a school for poor children.

Bec Evie was away at one of those outdoorsy camps.

India Bec was up the coast with uni friends.

Bec When they told us, we all headed home.

India By the time the three sisters were together again for their mum's funeral, they seemed kind of *separate* from each other.

We hold on the three sisters, desolate and separated from each other in space.

After a moment, MICHAELA and EVIE exit.

INDIA addresses the audience as if responding to heckles.

Look, I said no-one died in the *fire*. I didn't say this was a story where *no-one* ever died. There are risk factors pressing down on every single one of us every nanosecond.

Bec Sometimes a heinous thing can happen because one person's being a moron or a dickhead. Other times it's just a random event. The wrong kind of luck.

India For example, did you know that at any one time, ten per cent of the population carry the meningococcal bacterium in their throats? Did you know that the voltage in a cloud-to-ground lightning strike is one hundred million to one billion volts?

Bec India, you'll freak people out with your creepy stats.

BEC walks offstage.

India [*to the audience*] Okay. I think that's all the background data you need to know so we can get into it. [*She trains binoculars onto the Conway house.*] Remember: Michaela was desperate to study. I could see she had an elevated cortisol levels from stress.

Scene Two

The Conway house.

MICHAELA methodically lays out coloured folders for each subject she is studying. She sets two travel alarm clocks.

Michaela [*to herself*] You can do this. You can catch up. Stick to the study schedule and there will be enough hours. [*She takes a shaky breath, clearly not convincing herself.*] You can do this.

EVIE comes into the room, tugging on shoes, heading for the door.

Evie See ya.

Michaela Hang on, where are you going?

Evie Westfield.

Michaela Well, what time are you—?

Evie I don't know! Whatever! Charlotte said I could meet up with them at Westfield.

Michaela What are you—?

Evie Finally, someone at my new school is letting me hang around with them. Cool people. And you want to wreck that, do you?

Michaela No, I'm just saying—

Evie Oh my God, Michaela, are you *trying* to be an appalling bitch?

Michaela Dad said he wanted me to look after you while he's away.

Evie You don't need to take care of me. I'm not a bubble-brain little kid. Anyway, you'll just be studying like a—like a study machine.

Michaela Well yeah, but I need to know—

Evie It's better for you if I don't hang around here like a bad smell.

EVIE grabs keys, phone, whatever, and heads for the door. On her way out, she passes BEC on her way in.

[*To BEC*] Thanks heaps for not showing up at Dad's wedding, dog-breath.

Bec Don't mention it, tragic try-hard little sister.

Once EVIE is gone, MICHAELA makes a show of concentrating on her study notes, but keeps glaring at BEC.

Michaela I can't believe you.

Bec And here it comes: the moral lecture from Ms Perfect.

Michaela Dad was really upset. You should've come to the wedding.

BEC shrugs.

Are you okay? You look terrible.

Bec That's why I'm here—to get your advice on how to live a more wild and crazy fun-filled life.

MICHAELA ignores BEC's sarcasm.

Michaela Really, is everything okay?

Bec I like my life, alright? I don't want a stinking *career path*. Just because I'm not a stressed-out achievement-freak measuring my value as a person by how many prizes and—

Michaela Okay. I've heard that speech before. Don't waste your breath.

> *MICHAELA puts on her mp3 earphones and goes back to looking at her study notes.*

India [*to the audience*] Isn't it fascinating how incompatible siblings can be? They share genetic material plus many early environmental factors, so you'd expect more similarities. It's one of the anomalies I'm considering studying in depth.

> *BEC finds two large boxes filled with unopened wedding presents. She tips them out onto the floor—various parcels in fancy white and silvery wrapping.*

Bec Look at it all. There are three other crates in the hall.

Michaela They didn't have time to open the presents after the wedding.

Bec Why do people want more *stuff* when they already have a houseful of shiny stuff?

Michaela Well, friends want to give nice presents at a wedding so—

Bec I do understand the concept of gift-giving.

Michaela Why do I bother talking to you? I just get a mouthful of nasty back. Don't talk to me.

> *MICHAELA grabs some study notes to go somewhere else. BEC starts tearing the wrapping off some of the presents.*

What are you doing?

Bec I might confiscate some of these. They've already got plenty of wine glasses and shit.

Michaela Come on, Bec, you can't do that—

> *INDIA enters from a side door, carrying a tray covered in science equipment: beakers full of coloured liquid connected with tubes, et cetera.*

Hi, India.

Bec Is she here again? Haven't you fixed that hole in the side fence yet?

Michaela [*whispering to BEC*] Be nice. She's lonely.

India I just finished setting up this experiment.

Michaela That's great.

> *INDIA puts the experiment gear on a table.*

India Thought you might like to see it.

Michaela Definitely. But actually, India, right now, I really need to—

India I'm going to use Tollen's reagent as a way of identifying if a given compound is an aldehyde or not. See this bit here?

> *Kindly, MICHAELA lets INDIA show her the experiment. Meanwhile BEC addresses the audience.*

Bec [*to the audience*] India is an only child. She hasn't been to a normal school since she was nine. Now she has tutors and does online university courses. You gotta feel sorry for that kid. [*To INDIA*] Hey, India, did you know someone published a book with the title *Raise Your IQ by Eating Gifted Children*?

Michaela Bec, if you're just going to say poisonous things to people, why don't you—?

*Nathalie Fenwick (left) as India and Xenia Goodwin as Michaela in the 2010 **atyp** production in Sydney. (Photo: Alex Vaughan)*

Bec I'm going. Don't panic. I'll leave you to study for the HSC in peace.

BEC gathers up a boxful of gifts she's taking. She's left a messy pile of scrunched-up wrapping paper and ribbons.

Michaela You can't just take those—oh.

MICHAELA stops mid-sentence—no point arguing with BEC. BEC exits.

India I could help you study, Michaela. I could test you on things.

Michaela Thanks but I just need to put my head down—on my own, undisturbed—and do the study.

India Oh. Okay.

INDIA looks a bit wretched and MICHAELA relents.

Michaela Look, India, you can hang around here as long as you stay really quiet and let me concentrate.

India Yep. Sure. Quiet as a mouse. Actually, did you know mice can be quite noisy animals depending on—?

MICHAELA throws her a look and INDIA falls silent. MICHAELA makes a shooshing gesture.

Michaela I need total peace and quiet if I'm going to get through the study I need to do.

MICHAELA takes a deep breath. The house is quiet for a second. She smiles.
A second later, there's a blast of noise as the doorbell rings, the phone rings, her mobile does a raucous ringtone, and one of the alarm clocks goes off with a shrill sound.

India What's that?

Michaela The alarm tells me when to switch from studying History to Maths. According to my study schedule.

MICHAELA slams off the alarm sound and goes to the door. Meanwhile INDIA answers the landline.

India Hello. The Conways' house. India from next door speaking. [*She listens, puzzled by what she's hearing on the phone.*] Sorry? I can't understand what you're—

*MICHAELA comes back from the front door with her friend
PETRA, also seventeen or eighteen. PETRA carries an armload of
textbooks and folders, plus a bag of food. She's earnest, tense, a
bit bossy.*

Petra   I knew you'd be going mental with stress about the exams. I
was worried about you. So I thought, 'Petra—you know what you
need to do? Go round to Michaela's house and study together.
Help keep each other calm.'

Michaela   Oh… that's nice of you, Petra, but you know, really—

India   [*pointing to the phone receiver*] I can't work out who this is.

Petra   With everything that's happened—your mum and now your
dad getting married—God, Michaela, you must feel like crap.
Don't underestimate the emotional load you're carrying.

Michaela   Well—y'know—I don't. But right now, I just need to—

India   Michaela? You better take this. I'm not even sure it's a person.
There's just a wailing noise. Like a sea lion in distress.

*MICHAELA goes to take the phone. PETRA signals that she's
going to put the food she brought in the fridge and exits.*

Michaela   [*on the phone*] Hello?

*She listens for a moment, confused. She and INDIA exchange a
look—what is going on?*

[*To INDIA*] It might be my friend Natalie. [*Into the phone*] Natalie? Is
that you? [*Pause.*] Hang on, take a deep breath. I can't understand
any of the words you're— [*Pause.*] Maybe if you can stop crying a
bit, you could tell me what's happened— [*Pause.*] Is this about the
exams? Are you stressed about the exams? [*Pause.*] Cameron said
what? He broke up with you? Oh, Nat, I'm so sorry.

*She stays on the phone, listening and occasionally responding
with 'oh no' or 'mmm'.*
*At the same time, PETRA comes back in, brandishing packets of
ham and cheese.*

Petra   Michaela, your fridge is a horror show. Ham—not even
free-range. I told you how they treat pigs for ham and bacon
production. Especially horrifying when you realise that pigs are
incredibly sensitive animals.

MICHAELA puts her hand over the receiver so she can answer PETRA.

Michaela I know and I'm—look, I don't do all the shopping in this house.

Petra I thought you were really listening, really starting to see why being vegan is the only humane choice.

Michaela Well, no—yeah—I mean, no, I am thinking about it—

Petra The egg industry depends on killing every male chicken that's born. So don't kid yourself that free-range makes it all sweet. The dairy industry involves terrible cruelty to cows and—hello—what do you think they do with all the male dairy cattle?

Michaela Yes, of course, it's something—

Petra It's not like I want to guilt-trip you or anything but—

Michaela No, no, you're right. And I do feel guilty. [*Into the phone*] Oh no, I wasn't talking to you then, Natalie. Could you just hang on a sec? Petra, could we maybe talk about this—?

The other alarm clock goes off with a sharp sound, making MICHAELA yelp with fright. INDIA switches it off.

Petra Oh my God, look at you. You're shaking. You are so stressed out. Poor baby. I'm going to make you some vegan donuts.

Michaela Oh, uh, thanks Petra, but really—

But PETRA is already heading for the kitchen.

Petra Did you know that some donut shops use a product made from duck feathers? But I found this great vegan recipe. We'll have a donut pigout and cheer ourselves up, yeah?

PETRA exits. MICHAELA is stranded on the phone.

Michaela No, Natalie, I don't think you should go round to his house and ram his mobile phone up his— [*Pause.*] Sorry, sorry if that sounded snappy. Calm down, Nat. What exactly did he say?

MICHAELA exits, still listening on the cordless phone, to follow PETRA into the kitchen.
INDIA creeps out of the scene to address the audience.

India Meanwhile, Michaela's little sister Evie caught the bus down to Westfield.

Scene Three

The shopping centre food court.

India Evie used to have excellent friends at her old school but she got sick of always being 'the girl whose mother died'. That's why she changed high schools. And that's why Evie was in the food court at Westfield, doing major sucking-up to girls from her new school.

EVIE hangs around with CHARLOTTE, a pretty and confident fifteen-year-old. CHARLOTTE is flanked by her two cronies: hard-faced KRISTIN and ALICE, who giggles but rarely speaks. All the girls are drinking Boost juices.

Charlotte Do you reckon you can feel the guarana affecting you yet?

Evie Yeah, I'm feeling a bit zingy.

Charlotte [*with a snort*] You feel 'zingy'?! I think that's just your imagination, Evie.

Kristin The whole guarana thing's probably bullshit.

Charlotte Totally. Just so they can suck more money out of suckers.

Alice [*giggling*] Suckers.

EVIE joins in the laughing, a bit too loudly.

Charlotte Evie's having a hellish weekend because of her dad's wedding. Hey, you don't mind if I tell Kristin and Alice about how your father married your old Geography teacher?

Kristin Aww, how gross.

EVIE takes a second to recover from the shock of CHARLOTTE telling and then responds a bit too loudly.

Evie Yeah. Gross.

Charlotte Poor old Evie.

Evie Well, y'know, it is kind of tough—I mean, seeing my dad get married to some other—

Charlotte [*with a snort*] You need to harden up, precious! My parents have been married three times each, counting once to each other. I think it's cool going to all those weddings. I've scored heaps of clothes that way.

Alice Oh! Like that blue one with the strappy bits! Which wedding was that for?

12

CHARLOTTE ignores ALICE and gets out her mobile.

Charlotte Do you guys want to see a photo of the rancid dress Evie had to wear to her dad's wedding?

Evie Oh, Charlotte, I really only meant for you to see that.

But it's too late. CHARLOTTE is already holding up her mobile to show the other two. They hoot and laugh. EVIE, playing along, laughs too loudly.

Yeah, I know. Hideous.

Charlotte Hey. Hey. Hey. You know what we should do to cheer Evie up? Get her some decent dresses.

Evie Oh thanks, but I don't really have any money so—

Charlotte Only boring people need money to go shopping.

Evie Sorry? I don't—oh…

Charlotte I know how to get the security tags off the designer stuff.

Kristin My record is four seconds.

Evie But don't they also have security cameras or something?

From left: Claudia Brooks as Charlotte, Lucy Freyer as Alice and Amy Mitchell as Kirstin in the 2010 **atyp** production in Sydney.
(Photo: Alex Vaughan)

13

Charlotte That's why it works best if *we* take the tags off the clothes and then *you* put them in your bag and walk out.

Alice That really confuses the security guys.

Kristin Who are all brain-damaged meatheads anyway.

Alice [*giggling*] Brain-damaged meatheads.

Charlotte Yes yes yes, I'm liking this plan. We pick out some decent clothes for poor Evie plus we harvest a few extra dresses.

Evie Extra ones?

Charlotte To sell to people at school for cash.

Evie Oh.

Charlotte Don't you reckon it's unfair that only rich people can afford really cool clothes?

Evie I guess…

Charlotte It's totally unfair. So we can redistribute fashion to people who need it for half-price.

Evie You guys have done this before?

Charlotte We do it all the time.

Alice Heaps.

Kristin It's a much better rate of pay than shovelling fries at McDonald's.

> ALICE giggles. EVIE is panicky, not sure what to say.

Charlotte Oh my God, I think Evie's having a major guilty spazz-attack.

Kristin 'Ooh, I can't steal anything.'

Charlotte Look, don't you reckon these big shops make heaps of money by ripping people off?

Evie I guess…

Charlotte So we're just balancing it up.

Kristin And if they're too stupid to suss how easy it is to nick stuff…

Charlotte Exactly. They deserve to have stuff nicked. [*She waggles her empty drink cup, irritated.*] How come they always put the bins so far away?

Evie Oh—oh, I'll take those.

> EVIE gathers up the other girls' empty drink cups and dashes over to a bin. She uses this opportunity to take a deep breath and try to think clearly.
> Meanwhile, CHARLOTTE shows the other two the photo on her mobile again.

Charlotte Hang on, is that a photo of a hippo in a really rank formal dress?

Kristin Don't blame the dress. She'd look like a hippo whatever.

Charlotte Kristin, that is not true. You are a heinous bitch.

When EVIE comes back the other three are whispering and laughing.

Anyway, we're going shopping with our special five-finger discount.

Evie What's a five-finger discount?

ALICE waggles her fingers and giggles.

Charlotte So, Evie, you can come with us and get some clothes if you like. But if it freaks you out and, y'know, you can't handle it, that's cool.

EVIE hesitates for a second. KRISTIN whispers something to ALICE who splutters into giggles.

Evie Uh, I'll—yeah, I'll come.

Charlotte Cool.

INDIA appears, directing the audience to the next scene.

India Meanwhile, down the street, Bec was doing some special shopping of her own.

Scene Four

A suburban shopping street.

BEC walks along the street with a plastic bag from a chemist. Maybe she pulls a packet out of the bag to read the instructions on the box before slipping it back into the bag.

She looks distracted, not sure which direction to go.

A MARKET RESEARCHER spots BEC wandering in her direction. The RESEARCHER is friendly and smiley. She could have a fold-out table with display boxes of chocolate samples.

Researcher Hi! We're conducting some consumer research for Sweetheart Chocolates. Would you be able to spare ten minutes of your time to answer a few questions?

Bec Sorry? Oh look, I don't think—

Researcher After the questionnaire, you get to taste test a lot of chocolate.

Bec Free choccies. Yeah, why not? I got nowhere else to be for the next ten minutes.

Researcher Great! It's really hard to get people. So thanks. [*Consulting her clipboard*] I have to ask you this statistical blahblah first. One: age group. I'm guessing you're either in fifteen-to-nineteen or twenty-to-twenty-five.

Bec Well, I'm twenty—but, God 'twenty-to-twenty-five' sounds so grown-up. I'm not that grown-up.

The RESEARCHER laughs, filling in the form, not noticing that BEC is actually quite rattled.

Researcher Marital status?

Bec Not married. My father married my little sister's Geography teacher yesterday. Is there room for that on your form?

Researcher [*laughing*] No. It's *your* marital status. Should I tick the box for 'single' or 'in a long-term relationship'?

Bec My long-term boyfriend dumped me on Thursday night. [*Getting out her mobile*] I can ring Tom and ask him if he really meant it when he said I was 'a moody, paranoid mental case'.

The RESEARCHER laughs nervously, feeling awkward in the face of BEC's emotional intensity.

Researcher No thanks. Don't worry. Next one: income bracket. The form has a few categories you can—see?

She flips the clipboard around to show BEC. BEC is fighting tears.

Bec Well, I lost my job this morning so I guess my in—

Researcher Oh, I should say, this form is confidential. I mean, your name won't ever be—

Bec Income is zero dollars. So tick that one: 'less than 5,000 dollars per year'.

Researcher Right—uh: level of education. Secondary, tertiary, post-graduate.

Bec I bombed out of uni. Law degree. You get the HSC marks and everyone reckons—but Law is so boring it shrivels your eyeballs and—oh, you know what? I bang on about Law being boring but really, it was me. I stuffed up. Completely stuffed up uni. Even failed the Arts subjects.

The RESEARCHER hands BEC a tissue.

Researcher Listen, umm, we can stop doing this if you—
Bec No, keep going. I've got to earn the free chocolates. Next one?
Researcher How many people live in your household?
Bec What?
Researcher It's so people can say if they have kids or live with their parents or in a share house or whatever.

BEC looks wretched.

We can skip that one.
Bec My dad just got married—oh, I told you that already. My little sisters hate my guts. With good reason. Mum died—year and a half ago. I got evicted from my house this morning. And now there's a chance I might be pregnant. [*She shows the pregnancy test kit inside her chemist bag.*] So put down 'homeless potential single mother'.

BEC looks even more wretched. The RESEARCHER reaches out to pat BEC's arm, awkward but kind. BEC smiles her thanks and then points to the clipboard— 'keep going'.

Researcher Oh well, there's just a few multiple choice ones. Which answer best describes your feelings. When I've had a really bad day, I like to: (a) pamper myself with a bubble bath and a pedicure; (b) treat myself to my favourite chocolate or other sweet indulgence; or (c) spend time with my family and loved ones.

The RESEARCHER looks up to see that BEC is so wretched she can't speak. The RESEARCHER scoops up handfuls of chocolate samples and pours them into BEC's chemist bag.

Bec Thanks.
Researcher You're welcome.

BEC wanders off with the chocolates.

India [*to the audience*] Back at the Conways' house, the phone kept ringing but Michaela let the machine take it. It was Evie Conway trying to get through on the phone. She needed to talk to Michaela.

Scene Five

The back office of a department store.

EVIE is perched on a chair, terrified. She's been crying and holds a fistful of screwed-up tissues. She dials various numbers on her mobile but without success.

Evie [*into the phone*] Hi. It's Evie. If you're there, pick up. Oh... anyway, I'm at Westfield. Not in the actual shops. I'm in an office place out the back of the shops. Could you—it's hard to explain. Could you call me back?

> *A STORE SECURITY PERSON enters. Early twenties, officious and defensive.*

Store Security Person Did you get through to your parents?

Evie I don't want to bother my dad. He's on his honeymoon.

Store Security Person This is a charming wedding present. His daughter gets caught stealing.

> *EVIE dissolves into tears. The STORE SECURITY PERSON sighs and briskly hands her a box of tissues.*

I have to keep a supply of tissues in here. You thieving girls can always turn on the waterworks.

Evie Sorry?

Store Security Person Look, is there some other responsible adult you can ring to come down here?

Evie I tried my auntie but she's not there. My sister Michaela—she's not answering the phone either.

Store Security Person Keep trying.

> *EVIE starts typing a text.*

Evie This is the first time ever in my life I've stolen anything.

Store Security Person Yeah? It's amazing how many people we catch shopstealing for 'the first time ever'.

Evie Really?

Store Security Person No. Do I look stupid to you?

Evie Pardon? No.

Store Security Person I'm not stupid. A person can perform at the top level in retail management without being the person who got the academic prizes year after year.

EVIE gives up on the phone.

Evie I'm so sorry for what I did. Is there any way you could… I don't know…

Store Security Person You princesses think you're much cleverer than everyone around here.

Evie I don't. I don't think—

Store Security Person You know a trick to get security tags off the items, do you?

Evie Uh—yeah.

The STORE SECURITY PERSON scrutinises EVIE.

Store Security Person You're a shocking liar. I bet you haven't got a clue about it. You've got accomplices who get the tags off.

Evie Accomplices… that makes it sound like a bank robbery or something.

Store Security Person Hey. You stole more than nine hundred bucks worth of clothes.

Evie Nine hundred? Oh…

Store Security Person So, the system is your co-criminals take the tags off, then walk out. You slip the merchandise in your bag and you all meet up outside the store to divide the stolen goods?

EVIE shrugs, fighting tears.

Bad luck for you—you were the trained monkey who got caught.

EVIE can't meet the STORE SECURITY PERSON's gaze. She focusses on her mobile, trying to call again.

And I bet there's no way you'll dob in your friends.

EVIE shakes her head.

Do you reckon those friends would be so loyal to you if they were the ones sitting here?

EVIE shrugs.

Well, I am going to have to ring the police.

Evie The police? Do you have to?

Store Security Person That's store policy.

India [*to the audience*] Evie kept trying to ring Michaela for help. But Petra had switched off Michaela's mobile.

Scene Six

The Conway house.

INDIA is watching the house through binoculars.

MICHAELA lies flat on her back on the floor. PETRA prowls the room, bossing her around.

Petra The thing is, Michaela, you *must* relax. We desperately need to chill out if we're going to get through this exam ordeal. That's why I decided, 'Petra, turn off your mobile. Unplug yourself and get calm.'

Michaela Well, yeah, I can see—

Petra Don't let your camomile tea get cold.

Michaela Oh. Yeah.

> *MICHAELA hoists herself up awkwardly on one elbow so she can sip from a mug of tea which is on the floor beside her.*

Petra Camomile tea is excellent for relaxing the stress centres in the body.

> *The phone rings again. MICHAELA goes to get up.*

Michaela I should answer it this time. It's probably Natalie. She sounded really upset before.

Petra Let whoever it is leave a message.

> *The ringing stops as the phone switches to message.*

You've got to think about *you* now, Michaela. Last night, I ended up in a complete state. 'Oh my God, Petra, you're behind in Maths, your English is a pile of poo.' But then I thought, 'Come on, Petra, you can get through this by breathing, eating right, supporting each other as friends'.

Michaela That sounds great and I really appreciate—I just wonder if I'd feel less stressed if I got up off the floor and looked at my study notes.

Petra I can hear the tension in your voice. Close your eyes. Use this wheat bag.

> *She hands MICHAELA a small wheat bag to cover her eyes once she's lying down again.*

I'm going to get you relaxed. Cook you up some yummy donuts. And *then* we might be ready to do some actual study.

Michaela [*her eyes covered by the bag*] Well… y'know… I am starting to feel a bit more relaxed.

Petra Excellent.

PETRA leaves the room.

INDIA enters, bringing her science experiment paraphernalia with her. She sees MICHAELA lying on the floor, eyes closed, so creeps in quietly.

MICHAELA keeps talking, assuming the person who came into the room was PETRA.

Michaela Y'know, Petra, the other day, I had this fantasy about bolting out of the HSC exam room and running away. Do you reckon it's a premonition I'll have a total meltdown?

She laughs nervously and waits for PETRA to reply. But PETRA is out of the room.

You're right. Just ignore me. Why do I get so anxious? I try to make everything perfect or—or—it's like I can hear the whole universe humming at me like a bomb about to go off—except I don't know which bit of my life is about to explode. And then my head starts spinning and I have to make things be still and solid for a minute. I try to do things I can be *certain* about—I can get good school results, I can raise the money for the poor kids, I can keep the people in this house safe. Do you get what I mean, Petra?

No answer.

But do I just look like an idiot—flapping around like a headless chicken? Oh, sorry, for a vegan 'a headless chicken' is a horrible image, eh. Petra?

India Umm… she can't hear you.

MICHAELA takes the wheat bag off and sits up.

Michaela India. Hello.

India She's in the kitchen cooking, I think.

Michaela Did you hear me rabbitting on then like a—

India Rabbitting like a chicken?

21

Michaela Lying on the floor with a bag of muesli on my face talking crap out loud to nobody.

India Not nobody. I was listening. Actually, I've been reading some amazing material about chaos theory and random events and how neurological studies of—

Michaela Y'know, India, sometime I'd love to hear your views about the random nature of existence. But right now, I just need to study 2-unit Maths. [*She checks her watch.*] Oh Christ, my study schedule's gone down the toilet! I'm never going to get through—oh God, oh God, oh God… [*She scrambles to get some study folders together.*] India, can you say I've gone for a walk? I'm going to hide in the bathroom and go over my notes, okay?

India Okay, but I must warn you I'm not a very convincing liar.

Michaela Well, do your best.

> *MICHAELA sneaks out with an armload of folders.*
> *The phone rings and INDIA answers it.*

India Hello. This is the Conway house. India from next door speaking. Oh hi, Evie. No, Michaela's gone for a walk. I can give

*Nathalie Fenwick as India in the 2010 **atyp** production in Sydney. (Photo: Alex Vaughan)*

her a message if you— [*Pause.*] Okay. Try her mobile. 'Bye.

The doorbell rings. INDIA goes to the front door just as PETRA re-enters from the kitchen, wiping her hands on a tea towel.

Petra Yummy, yummy. The donuts won't be long. It took a while to get the oil hot enough.

We can hear NATALIE sniffling before she even gets into the room. NATALIE is the same age as MICHAELA and PETRA.

Natalie Michaela! Can you believe I took that piece of scum back and now he dumps me again?

Petra Hi, Nat. I heard what happened. Cameron's not good enough for you. He's a steaming piece of—

Natalie Thanks, babe. Where's Michaela?

India She's gone for a walk.

Petra Really? Oh. The donuts'll be ready soon.

PETRA runs back to the kitchen.

Natalie [*to INDIA*] You're the brainy kid from next door, right?

India Right.

Natalie Have you got a boyfriend?

India No. I mean, I haven't even gone through puberty yet so boys aren't really—

Natalie Good. Keep it that way.

India What? You mean don't go through puberty? From a hormonal point of view, that would be—

Natalie I'm saying don't ever get a boyfriend. They destroy you as a person. Remember that.

India Okay.

The phone rings. INDIA goes to answer it.

Natalie If that's Cameron—if he's trying to track me down—tell him to go and stick his head up a dead bear's bum.

India Umm—okay. Hello. The Conways'.

Natalie Actually, give me the phone.

She grabs the phone from INDIA.

Cameron? Is that you? Cam? [*She puts the phone down.*] Hung up. I'm pretty sure it was him. It sounded like his breathing. Oh God…

This reduces NATALIE to more weeping.

The smoke alarm beeps in the kitchen, then a moment later switches off again.

MICHAELA hurries into the room, her arms full of study notes.

Michaela What was that? Was that the smoke alarm?

Natalie Michaela! There you are!

MICHAELA yelps with surprise to see NATALIE and feels caught out. She drops the notes she's holding, scattering them across the floor.

Michaela Oh, Nat… I didn't know you were here.

PETRA pops her head into the room.

Petra Don't worry about the smoke alarm. I've fixed it.

Michaela Well, Petra, what are you—you shouldn't really—

But PETRA has ducked back to the kitchen.
MICHAELA scrambles to pick up the papers. INDIA helps her, stacking pages right next to her science experiment.

Natalie Thanks for letting me come over, Michaela. You're the one friend I need to talk to about this.

Michaela Sure, of course you can—just give me a sec to get this stuff—

Natalie I can *feel* my heart aching. I mean, inside my chest, there is an actual physical ache where my heart is.

India That pain is probably psychosomatic or else originating in your digestive tract. It's a common misconception that the heart is—

MICHAELA signals to INDIA—'don't pursue this now'.

Michaela Yeah, you must be feeling terrible, Nat. I mean, breaking up is always hard but Cameron picked a shocking time to—

Natalie And he said truly hurtful things to me.

Michaela Oh, that's even worse. No-one deserves that.

Natalie You're the only person who understands what I'm going through.

Michaela Why don't you go and have a lie-down in Bec's old room and then later we can—?

NATALIE has pulled a photo of Cameron out of her bag and stares at it, touching his face.

24

Natalie Why doesn't Cameron realise we're perfect for each other? He's so sweet. He's so amazing.

NATALIE collapses onto the photo, weeping (or whatever).

Michaela Can I smell something burning?

PETRA pops her head in again.

Petra I overcooked the first batch. Next batch will be perfect.

MICHAELA holds the crumpled jumble of study notes in one hand and pats her weeping friend with the other.

India [*to the audience*] Back at Westfield, Evie sat for another hour waiting for Michaela.

Scene Seven

EVIE is in the office alone, wretched and frightened. She has a pile of scrunched-up tissues in her lap. She shoves some of them into her pockets.
The STORE SECURITY PERSON enters.

Store Security Person Apparently your sister's at the front office. Big relief, eh?

Evie Yeah, but—oh… Michaela's gonna be so mad with me.

Store Security Person I need to have a chat with her. You stay here.

EVIE nods obediently.
We leave EVIE sitting there alone as the STORE SECURITY PERSON walks into the front office to meet BEC.

Bec Hi. Sorry it's taken a while for someone to get down here—

Store Security Person Much later and I'd be forced to send her off in a police wagon.

Bec Right, of course. Sorry. So what do I need to do now?

Store Security Person Well, your sister was apprehended with over nine hundred dollars worth of merchandise.

Bec Nine hundred? Far out… Listen, Evie's not the kind of kid who—

Store Security Person We get packs of shoplifters in here.

Bec Yeah, I can imagine.

Store Security Person They think everyone who works here is a visually-impaired idiot.

Bec I get what you're saying. They don't understand how things work.

Store Security Person Exactly. We have sophisticated security systems but these little princesses still think they can fool us.

Bec Must be so frustrating for you.

Store Security Person It is. They work in teams stealing lists of items on order.

Bec Yeah? Wow... But my little sister, she's not some experienced shoplifter. This is a stupid one-off mistake. Is there any chance you could let this one go?

Store Security Person If she told us the names of her co-offenders, we might consider it.

Bec I understand how that would help. But you know kids like Evie never dob on their mates.

Store Security Person True. They don't.

Bec You're a smart person. You get what kind of girl Evie is.

Store Security Person I'm pretty sure she was talked into something by more experienced girls.

Bec Yeah. You can suss out what's happened.

Store Security Person I can make an intelligent guess.

Bec For sure. Thing is, our father's away and I don't want to lay a big family sob story on you, but—you can imagine. Is there any way you could use your discretion and let her off with—I don't know—a warning or something?

Store Security Person It's store policy to lay formal charges with the police.

Bec But are you allowed to use your professional judgement about this one?

The STORE SECURITY PERSON pulls a face, considering it.

Store Security Person I've started the paperwork, but I suppose I can bin that. You can take your sister home as long—

Bec I'll make sure she's got the message. Thank you so much.

The STORE SECURITY PERSON pulls a stern face, indicates the room where EVIE is waiting, then exits.
EVIE is surprised to see BEC walk in.

Evie Oh... Bec.

Bec Der. You left a message on my phone.

Evie I thought you'd tell Michaela and she'd—

Bec Bad luck, you got me.

Evie Have you talked to—?

Bec How stupid are you? We're talking serious shit here. Juvenile offenders court, good behaviour bonds, all that stuff.

    EVIE dissolves into tears again.

  Unbelievable. I thought you were an annoying little worm, but not a moron.

Evie I just wanted to be normal and have friends and hang out with—I just wanted to be normal.

Bec And normal is stealing hundreds of bucks worth of designer label clothes, is it?

Evie No...

Bec Far out... And these 'friends'—do you reckon they might actually be a swarm of bitches who were using you? Using you— the dopey new girl—because they can sniff out how desperate you are to impress them?

Evie Really, Bec, don't hold back. Don't be nice to me right now when I already feel like crawling into a hole and never coming out.

Bec Yeah, well...

    BEC shakes her head and they sit in silence for a second.

Evie I wish Mum was here.

Bec This stuff would be hard even if Mum was around.

Evie What stuff? You mean, getting caught shoplifting?

Bec I mean, all of it—friends, school, life, all of it. Believe me, it wasn't a whole lot easier even before.

Evie Well, I don't know.

Bec Anyway, I bet Mum wouldn't've been able to talk you out of trouble like I just did.

Evie What?

Bec Mrs Testy-pants in the other room is letting you go without police charges.

    The good news makes EVIE dissolve into tears and grab for more tissues.

Evie Really? She's really—? Oh my God, thanks, Bec.

Bec I didn't even have to play the Dead Mother card.

BEC walks out with EVIE gathering up the piles of tissues and hurrying after her.
INDIA addresses the audience.

India Back at the Conway house, things were getting wobbly because—Oh-oh, hang on, before we go back there, you might enjoy seeing what happened when Bec and Evie were on their way out of Westfield.

Scene Eight

Westfield.
BEC stalks through the shops with EVIE scurrying behind her.

Evie You don't have to take me. I can catch a bus on my own.
Bec I'm going to deposit you at home before you do anything else diabolically stupid.
Evie You don't have to treat me like crap just because—

BEC turns around to glare at EVIE.

Okay. Sorry. And thank you. You were amazing and I'm—oh…

EVIE has spotted someone.

Bec What?
Evie It's Charlotte. In front of the movie poster. Quick, let's—oh no, she's seen me.

EVIE waves limply as CHARLOTTE enters.

Charlotte There you are! So what happened? We saw the security guard grab you but then we—
Evie You saw what happened to me? And you just left?
Bec Of course she dumped you and ran.
Charlotte [*to BEC*] Who are you?
Evie My sister. Bec.
Charlotte Well, Bec, there was nothing we could have done, so don't give me that face, okay? I bet they just gave you a big lecture and let you go.
Evie Sort of.
Charlotte So it's cool. Those security people are retards. Tragic cases too dumb to pass the police test. I knew you'd be okay.

Evie If Bec hadn't come and talked to the—

Charlotte You didn't give them my name, did you?

Evie No.

Charlotte If you did—well, it wouldn't be good. It wouldn't be good for you at school. If you get me.

Evie I didn't dob.

CHARLOTTE smiles and switches back into chatty girl mode.

Charlotte Great. Hey, guess why I'm stuck here? It's my stepbrother's birthday and Dad's making me sit through some lame little-kid movie and have dinner with them. Poor me. Ooh, maybe I could get out of it by telling Dad you got caught for shoplifting and you're really upset.

Evie Sorry?

Charlotte You are upset, aren't you?

Evie Yes.

Charlotte So as your friend, I need to comfort you instead of going to the stupid movie, right?

EVIE is speechless for a moment.

Bec Evie, could you get me a bottle of water from the place round the corner?

EVIE nods, shaken, and exits.
Once she's gone, BEC steps right up to CHARLOTTE and backs her into a wall. With one swift movement, BEC grabs CHARLOTTE's wrists with one hand and clamps the other hand around her throat.

Don't try yelling out. If anyone comes over I'll just laugh and say we were joking around.

Charlotte You're a mental case.

Bec Well, many people share that opinion. I know who you are.

Charlotte What? You don't—

BEC tightens her grip slightly on CHARLOTTE's neck. CHARLOTTE is now too scared of her to talk back.

Bec Unlike my trusting little sister, I know exactly the species of poisonous, using bitch you are. Leave Evie alone so she can find some decent friends. Don't spread any stories or rumours about

29

her. I happen to know lots of people at your school and I will find out what goes on. You would be amazed how a few phone calls can stuff up a person's life.

Charlotte You're full of crap. What could—?

Bec Oh, Charlotte… don't call my bluff. Evie's a sweet kid. Myself, I'm not sweet. I can be vicious and I can let things get way out of proportion. I don't seem to care about my reputation or my future. Which makes me very dangerous to a creature like you. Leave Evie alone. Fair enough?

CHARLOTTE nods. BEC lets her go.

Enjoy the movie.

CHARLOTTE hurries off, terrified. BEC exits.

India [*to the audience*] Yeah. How about that? Heavy. So, as I was saying, back at the Conway house, Michaela wasn't getting a whole lot of study done. Oh—I was using ironic understatement there—in case that wasn't clear. She wasn't getting *any* study done.

Scene Nine

The Conway house.

MICHAELA and NATALIE enter from the bathroom. MICHAELA is looking after NATALIE who has her head tipped back, with a wad of bloody tissues from a nosebleed.

Natalie I always get a nosebleed when I cry this much.

Michaela Come and sit down. Maybe watch some TV to take your mind off it.

PETRA enters from the kitchen with a fistful of MICHAELA's study notes. She stares ahead like a wallaby frozen in headlights, all her former confidence vanished.

Petra While I was waiting for the oil to get hot, I looked at your study notes, Michaela.

INDIA enters from the kitchen.

India Umm, excuse me—should donuts be that colour?

PETRA doesn't hear, lost in her own panic.

Petra I just realised I'm going to fail everything. I know nothing about Modern History. I don't know when anything happened in the world or why.

Michaela Petra, that's not true. You did fine in the trials and you—

Petra I can't remember any French words. Not one word. [*She observes a few study pages fall from her hands onto the floor.*] What's the French word for rug? I can't even remember the French word for rug!

India '*Le tapis*'.

> *PETRA looks at a page of Maths in her hand.*

Petra And Maths. I hate numbers. How can I pass Maths when I hate all numbers?

Michaela Come on, you'll be okay—

Petra What's the French word for number?

India '*Le nombre*'. Unless you mean a number in a series, which is '*le numero*'.

> *PETRA glances at INDIA with renewed panic. MICHAELA signals to INDIA to shut up.*

Petra I can't remember Maths or French or History. I'm going to fail. I'm going to fail. It's hopeless.

> *She lets the rest of the study notes drop from her hand and reveals that under those, she's holding a packet of ham. She rips open the packet and starts shoving slices of ham into her mouth.*

India I thought she was a vegan.

Michaela She is.

India Well, isn't ham against the rules if someone is a—?

> *MICHAELA signals to INDIA to shut up.*

Michaela Petra. Put the ham back in the fridge. Step away from the ham. I mean, you can have it if you want, but you'll feel better if you don't eat any more.

> *PETRA keeps shoving ham in her mouth.*
> *Meanwhile, NATALIE has found the photo of Cameron and is staring at it.*

Natalie You know what? I'm the one who's going to fail the HSC. Because of Cameron. Because he picked this week to break up with me and destroy me as a person so I can't study. He's a bastard. He's lower than pond scum. [*She finds a box of matches and lights one. She holds the match under the photo.*] He deserves to burn in hell for what he's done to me.

Michaela Nat, what are you doing? Be careful!

> *NATALIE sets fire to a corner of the photo and holds it, watching it burn. MICHAELA grabs a metal wastepaper bin and places it under the burning photo.*

Natalie Burn, you scummy bastard. How dare he do this to me! If I fail, it's going to be his fault.

> *PETRA stumbles out to the kitchen.*

Petra [*yelling from the kitchen*] The donuts are burned! Ruined.

> *NATALIE relishes watching Cameron's photo burn and then drops the last bit into the metal bin.*
> *PETRA re-enters with a can of whipped cream and sprays cream directly into her mouth, swallowing down big gulps.*

India Umm—should you be eating cream? That's a dairy product and I thought vegans weren't supposed to eat any—

Petra I've already eaten ham. So what the hell...

> *She sprays more cream into her mouth. INDIA watches her, fascinated.*
> *Meanwhile, NATALIE has picked up her mobile.*

Natalie Oh! Michaela! Cameron texted me! 'Call me'! He wants me to call! Should I call? I don't know if should call. Maybe I'll just text 'Why should I call?' And see if he calls me.

> *Breathless with excitement, NATALIE punches in a text, then stares at the phone, willing it to ring.*
> *MICHAELA takes the metal bin away from NATALIE.*
> *PETRA lets the cream canister drop from her hand and plonks herself on the floor in despair.*

Petra What am I doing?

> *PETRA stares into space like a zombie.*

Michaela Are you okay, Petra?

Petra No. I'm not okay. I feel sick. I feel terrible. I hate myself.

MICHAELA can see that PETRA is seriously upset. She sits beside her on the floor and puts an arm around her.

Michaela Listen, it's not that bad. Remember how much you usually—

Petra I know you all think the whole veganism thing is just Petra being a wanker.

Michaela I don't.

Petra But it's something I've researched and thought about. I believe certain things about the rights of animals and if I follow those things through logically, there's only one decision I can make. This is a real thing for me.

Michaela I know that. Well... maybe I didn't know that for sure. But I know it now you've told me.

*Ines English as Petra in the 2010 **atyp** production in Sydney. (Photo: Alex Vaughan)*

Petra Is it better to be someone who doesn't believe anything and just does whatever is easy and comfy? Is it ridiculous to believe passionately in something and try to follow that?

Michaela It's not ridiculous. Good on you for working out what you believe and sticking to—

PETRA gives a teary laugh.

Petra But what kind of tragic vegan am I? Dairy and ham. Ham!

Michaela It was one time. And you were upset. Don't beat yourself up.

MICHAELA gives PETRA a reassuring squeeze.

India [*to MICHAELA*] Oh, umm, before—when you were hiding in the bathroom, pretending to be out for a walk—Evie rang. She said she'd leave a message on your mobile.

Michaela Oh. Okay.

MICHAELA leaves PETRA to pick up her mobile and listen to voicemail.
Meanwhile, NATALIE has dialled and is talking on her mobile.

Natalie Cameron. When you get this message, don't call me. I can't speak to you right now. I mean, I've got the exams to worry about and—well, those things you said really cut me and I... I wonder how you'll feel when you hear my voice on this message... I wonder if you think—I mean, I thought things were going really awesome with us and— [*Fighting tears*] Anyway. Just don't call me. 'Bye.

MICHAELA puts down her phone, stunned.

Michaela I've got to get to Westfield. [*She grabs her bag and yanks shoes on her feet.*] My little sister's been arrested for shoplifting.

India What? Who?

Michaela Evie. She's waiting for me. I didn't know. Oh God, oh God.

She rushes towards the front door just as BEC and EVIE enter.

There you are. I only just heard your message. I thought you were under arrest. I thought—

Bec I went down there. It's sorted out.

Michaela [*to EVIE*] How could you be such an idiot?! Did you really steal something? I can't believe it! What were you—?

Bec Michaela, stop. She's already had a hard time today.

MICHAELA shakes her head in disbelief, about to say something, when BEC makes a 'stop' gesture.

She's a good kid and you know that. Everyone makes dumb mistakes sometimes. Most of us do anyway. So give her a break, yeah?

MICHAELA hesitates, still trying to get her head around this. EVIE is staring at BEC, amazed that she stuck up for her.

Michaela Well—uh—are you okay? Are you going to tell me what happened?

Evie Don't tell Dad. Please. We don't have to tell Dad, do we?

Michaela I guess not.

EVIE goes over and empties fistfuls of screwed-up tissues out of her pockets and dumps them in the metal bin with the burnt photo. MICHAELA leaves her be for now.

Bec What is that burny smell?

Michaela We tried to cook donuts but they didn't work out.

Bec Evie, turn on the ceiling fan, will you? See if we can clear that horrible smell.

She takes in the chaos in the room, including sniffling NATALIE and desolate PETRA on the floor.

[*To MICHAELA*] And have you got any study done with all this going on?

Michaela Not a lot.

Bec What exactly is wrong with them?

India [*meaning NATALIE*] Well, her boyfriend—who is lower than pond scum—destroyed her as a person. Because of him, she's going to fail the HSC.

Her description reduces NATALIE to even more helpless weeping.

[*Pointing out PETRA*] That one hates numbers and can't remember any French words so she's going to fail the HSC. That's why she ate ham. And half a can of cream—

PETRA nods miserably at INDIA's explanation.

35

—even though vegans aren't supposed to eat any animal products including eggs, milk or honey. And in fact ham is a big deal for a vegan because most pork production is especially cruel to pigs.

PETRA is so distressed she is now crying again, along with NATALIE.

Meanwhile, EVIE has slumped on the couch exhausted, shoving some of MICHAELA's notes onto the floor, adding to the mess.

INDIA has picked up the whipped cream and is reading the writing on the can.

BEC and INDIA both talk simultaneously at MICHAELA.

Did you know that they put seaweed in whipped cream to make it viscous? Well, not unprocessed seaweed but alginates which are made from kelp which is a kind of seaweed that comes from—

Bec Far out, Michaela, you can really pick some tragic types to hang out with. How come you always get yourself—?

MICHAELA suddenly screams loudly—purposeful and assertive—as if she's setting off a fire alarm. The others instantly shut up or stop crying and stare at her, surprised.

Michaela Enough. That's enough. I need peace and quiet. Natalie, Petra—go home. I'll talk to you guys tomorrow. India, you go home too. Evie, disappear and watch TV in Dad's room or make Bec take you to the movies or whatever. I am now going to do some study.

India [*to the audience*] But in fact, she didn't have the chance. Because that's when we discovered the house was on fire.

Maybe snap to a blackout, followed quickly by siren sounds, screaming, flashing lights. MICHAELA bundles everyone offstage, except INDIA.

Scene Ten

INDIA pulls down a white screen which covers as large an area of the stage as possible.

Like a lecturer, she uses a pointer to talk the audience through diagrams about the fire—PowerPoint or overhead-projector images. The images could look like technical drawings and photos from a textbook.

India We have good reason to believe the fire started in the kitchen.

On the screen we might see an architectural drawing of a kitchen floor plan and then a picture of a smoke alarm with a cross through it.

Petra had disconnected the smoke alarm, so there was no warning.

The MARKET RESEARCHER from the earlier scene enters, with clipboard, and takes on the role of fellow lecturer.

Researcher The fire took hold quickly. We can't show—

India What? Hang on a second. I'm the narrator. Do you think you can just walk on and start talking?

Researcher I'm only helping with this bit.

India This is unacceptable. You can't—

Researcher Because of my experience in market research, I'm good with information.

India But you're a really minor character. A cameo role, in fact.

The RESEARCHER smiles sweetly to INDIA and then addresses the audience.

Researcher Since this is a play, with a small budget, we obviously can't do the flames and billowing black smoke onstage.

On the screen, we may see images of house fires.

You'll have to rely on your imaginations and draw on mental images from movies and personal experience.

The STORE SECURITY PERSON from the department store enters, also with clipboard.
INDIA sighs—she gives up. These two have taken over her job.

Store Security Person Luckily no-one was injured in the fire.

Researcher Thanks to Michaela. She used to make the whole family do fire drills every three months.

Store Security Person The three Conway sisters guided everyone outside to the designated marshalling area safely.

Researcher We can never be entirely sure how the fire progressed.

Store Security Person My theory is this: the tissues Evie put in the bin came in contact with an ember from the burnt photo of Natalie's ex-boyfriend.

Researcher The ceiling fan blew a piece of burning tissue across to the saucepan of hot oil from Petra's vegan donuts.

Store Security Person The oil fuelled a major blaze in the kitchen.

Researcher The study notes strewn everywhere acted as fuel.

Store Security Person Thereby spreading the fire to the bunched-up wrapping paper from the wedding presents left on the floor by Bec.

Researcher This ignited the lounge room curtains.

Store Security Person The fire then spread across the room.

Researcher Until it reached India's science experiment.

Store Security Person Which contained several highly explosive chemicals.

Researcher It took the fire brigade some hours to get the blaze under control.

Store Security Person The interior of the house was almost entirely destroyed.

Researcher The roof collapsed.

Store Security Person And other structural damage is yet to be assessed.

India Yes, yes, okay. Shoo. You've had your moment. Shoo.

She hustles the RESEARCHER and the STORE SECURITY PERSON offstage.

The point is, it's fascinating how a series of minor, random factors can combine to create such a major outcome.

The RESEARCHER and STORE SECURITY PERSON smile politely to INDIA and exit.
INDIA flips up the screen to reveal:

Scene Eleven

The street. Night.
The stage is full of smoke (if possible!) and the spill of swirling red lights from a few metres away.
MICHAELA, EVIE and BEC are sitting together on the ground, watching their house burn. They have blankets wrapped around them.

Bec I didn't know a fire could spread that fast.

Michaela It's incredible, isn't it?

Evie Reckon.

Michaela I told Dad I'd take care of things while he was away this week. Within twenty-four hours, Evie gets arrested and the house burns down.

Bec The perfect daughter is not so perfect.

MICHAELA crumples into tears.

Michaela, I'm sorry. I was only joking.

Michaela No no, I'm not crying because you said—it's everything, really. I've stuffed things up.

Bec You haven't. What kind of stupid prawn are you? You're not responsible for the whole world.

Michaela Well, y'know, after Mum died, it felt like I had to hold it all together.

BEC puts an arm around MICHAELA.

Bec Look, we're okay.

MICHAELA shrugs.

Michaela Yes. [*Pause.*] I wish Mum was here.

The other two share that feeling and there's a moment of silence.

I wish I could go back to being a little kid getting looked after.

The other two think about this and nod.

Evie Now Dad's got married, I feel like an orphan. I know that sounds dumb.

Bec No. I feel like an orphan too.

INDIA enters.

India Michaela, I'm sorry if my science experiment chemicals were the main accelerants and caused the fire to spread.

Michaela Don't worry, India. It was bad luck. Not your fault.

India You're an extremely nice person, Michaela.

Michaela Well, thanks for saying so. [*She mock strangles herself and wails.*] I'll have to ring Dad.

Evie Do you have to tell him while he's on holidays?

Bec Are you suggesting we let him come home—no warning—and see that?

BEC indicates the house.

Michaela Anyway, I'll have to talk to him so we can get the insurance stuff organised.

Bec What do you reckon the new wife is going to say about this?

MICHAELA pulls a face and shrugs.

Do you like her?

Michaela Yeah. I reckon she's scared of us, about how to get on with us.

Evie Oh, yeah.

Michaela And just plain scared of Bec.

BEC does an evil cackle.

India I'm scared of you too.

Evie I can't stop thinking of Dad's new wife as my Geography teacher.

MICHAELA laughs to herself.

Bec What?

Michaela What was it like at the parent-teacher night? Do you reckon Dad was having a perv at her tits over the desk while he was discussing Evie's Geography marks?

BEC and MICHAELA laugh.

Evie Errgh… stop it! They met properly at that dinner party. Dad didn't hit on her at my school.

Bec Yeah yeah, Evie, we know. Michaela's just letting herself be a naughty bitch for one second.

Michaela Anyway, I like her. And at least Dad looks happier.

Bec Happiest I've seen him since Mum died.

The other two think about this and nod.

And let's face it—she does have great tits.

MICHAELA laughs and EVIE slaps her sisters.

Evie Stop it. You guys are disgusting.

Bec New Wife is only forty.

Michaela So? She's not that much younger than Dad.

Bec No, I mean, forty's still young enough to have a baby.

Evie Does she want a baby?

Bec Who knows?

Evie A baby with our dad?

Bec Der. Who else?

Evie Really? Are you sure she—?

Michaela Relax, Evie. Bec's just stirring you. We don't know.

Evie Actually, I'd like it—if Dad and her had a baby. It'd be fun.

The other two sisters consider this, then nod. It would be fun.

Bec I did a pregnancy test this afternoon.

Michaela Oh my God, Bec.

Evie A pregnancy test on who?

Bec [*to EVIE*] Are you really that stupid?

Evie I was just asking—

Bec On myself.

Michaela And?

Bec I'm not.

Michaela Oh, that's a relief.

Bec Yeah. Scary though. That'd really be the icing on the cake, eh. The exploding cake of me totally bombing out in life.

Michaela You said you liked your life.

Bec I lied.

Michaela You said you didn't want a career or a proper—

Bec I don't know what I want. I'm scared shitless.

Michaela I so believe you're going to be okay and have a brilliant life.

Bec Yeah? I'm glad you're so sure.

The three of them fall silent.

Michaela Look at our house.

Bec You've got a strong case for Special Consideration in the HSC. It's gotta be worth five UAI points.

Michaela The HSC, oh. All my notes are burned to a crisp.

Bec The computer's probably melted into a plastic sculpture.

Michaela And we're homeless.

MICHAELA groans and collapses forward.

Evie Remember that thing Mum used to do when I got in a state about something?

Bec Mrs Tragic.

BEC starts doing a tragic wailing and sobbing act. The other two join in, sobbing hysterically, gasping for breath, howling, hiccupping, clutching at each other. It gets more over the top until it dissolves into uncontrollable laughter. The three end up grinning and breathless.

India I wish I was your sister.

The Conway sisters probably don't hear INDIA say that. PETRA and NATALIE enter.

Petra Hi, Michaela. We're both incredibly sorry about what happened.

Natalie You lost all your study stuff because of us.

Michaela Come on, guys, it's not your fault.

Petra We've collected our notes in your subjects.

Natalie Plus I borrowed some from Rosie.

Petra Rosie got all band sixes last year. So we figured her notes would be really excellent.

PETRA hands over several folders of notes.

Michaela Thanks, guys. I really appreciate this.

Natalie There's a spare bed at our place if you—

Michaela Oh, I haven't even thought about—

India Wait. I talked to my mother. We've got several guest rooms at our house. All three of you could stay.

The sisters look at each other, not sure what to say. BEC takes charge.

Bec Great. Thanks, India.

Petra Ooh—I'm going to lend you guys clothes from my place.

Natalie I'll get some too.

Petra Back soon.

*PETRA and NATALIE rush off.
MICHAELA glances at the study notes, then puts them aside.*

Michaela I just thought—we've lost all our stuff from before. From when Mum was around.

Evie Oh, yeah.

Michaela Dad kept some of her clothes in the wardrobe.

42

Bec Burnt to a crisp now.

Evie What about that hideous seahorse ornament made out of seaweed?

Michaela Oh, yeah. Why did she buy that disgusting thing?

Bec Because it made her laugh her guts out every time she looked at it.

Michaela All our photos from before.

Evie Oh, yeah…

> *MICHAELA and EVIE contemplate this and it makes them both tearful.*

Bec Ah well, the burnout sister isn't as stupid as she looks. [*She reaches behind her and lifts over a big stack of photo albums and computer disks.*] I rescued these.

Evie Oh, wow!

Michaela Ha! Well done, Bec.

Bec Plus—today hasn't only been bad luck. I scored some free choccies.

> *She brings out the chemist bag and offers around the chocolates.*

They're a bit melted out of shape.

Michaela Still yummy though.

> *They all makes noises in agreement, mouths full of chocolate.*
>
> *The three sisters sit side by side, eating chocolates and flipping through photo albums.*
>
> *INDIA addresses the audience.*

India I can't tell you what happens to the Conway sisters in the future. I've studied the evidence for clairvoyance. It's a load of dog poo. But I can tell what happened in the next little while. Evie decided to go back to her old school and she's much happier there. [*She hesitates, embarrassed.*] Actually, I'm—uh—I'm enrolling at the same school as Evie next year. Bec bullied me into it. I dunno… we'll see. Michaela did her best in the HSC exams. Whatever the results, she's taking a gap year, to work in an orphanage in Africa. Bec's taken a job in Guatemala teaching English for six months. She sent me a piece of lava from the Acatenango volcano. So the Conway sisters are okay. For now. Because you can never know what's going to happen. I mean, space debris could fall on any one of us or some kind of viral epidemic could sweep the—

Bec Hey, kid. Enough of the freaky stuff. Shut up and eat this.

BEC chucks a chocolate to INDIA.

India Okay.

INDIA pops the chocolate in her mouth, then sits down next to the sisters to look at the photos with them.
Red fire truck lights sweep across them as the lights fade.

THE END

From left: Darcie Irwin-Simpson as Bec, Xenia Goodwin as Michaela, Nathalie Fenwick as India (behind) and Stephanie Jaja as Evie in the 2010 **atyp** *production in Sydney. (Photo: Alex Vaughan)*

Also available from Currency Press

Engine
Janis Balodis

' Engine is a stroke of genius.' *ArtsHub*

It's a few months since Stevie died in a car crash. Natasha, his 17-year-old sister, has had it with strangers hugging her and Grumpop has moved in till things are on an even keel again. Together, this unlikely duo of heroes do battle with the demons of their grief, as their family forges a new way forward as they learn to live with the tragedy.

Engine is a story of young people and cars. It's about fixing what's broken and celebrating life. It's a funny and moving roller-coaster ride that will break your heart and mend it.

ISBN 978 0 86819 889 7

Boy Overboard
Patricia Cornelius / Morris Gleitzman

A story of adventure, ball control and hope.

Jamal and Bibi have a dream. To lead Australia to soccer glory in the next World Cup. But first they must face landmines, pirates, storms and assassins. Can Jamal and his family survive their incredible journey and get to Australia?

Adapted for the stage by Patricia Cornelius from Morris Gleitzman's best-selling novel, Boy Overboard depicts a deeply human side of the 'asylum seekers' issue by following the journey of Jamal and Bibi from Afghanistan to Australia. Based on real life events, this is a moving play about young people overcoming the confusion of war, politics and the search for a safe haven.

ISBN 978 0 86819 807 1

Hitler's Daughter – the play
Adapted by Eva Di Cesare, Sandra Eldridge, Tim McGarry **from the novel by Jackie French**

Did Hitler's daughter exist?

Four country children waiting in the rain for the school bus take turns telling stories. In an unusual twist, Anna's story takes the children to Nazi Germany. An intriguing tale about Heidi, a young girl caught in the turmoil of World War II, whose father was one of the most dreaded men in history.

One of the children, Mark, becomes engrossed in Heidi's story. In his conversations with his friends, his teacher and with his parents, he explores the moral and ethical issues it raises.

This intriguing play poses powerful questions about a frightening period in history and forces us to examine moral issues in relation to society's fears and prejudices in a fresh, compelling light.

Monkey Baa received the 2006 APACA Drovers Award for Audience Development for their highly acclaimed production of *Hitler's Daughter*.

ISBN 978 0 86819 813 2

Thursday's Child – the play
Adapted by Eva Di Cesare, Sandra Eldridge, Tim McGarry **from the novel by Sonya Harnett**

Tin Flute was born on a Thursday. He is a reclusive child who is more at home in subterranean tunnels he digs under his family's farm than he is above ground. As his impoverished family struggles for survival in rural Australia during the Great Depression, Tin retreats further underground into a world of darkness and troubling secrets.

Adapted from Sonya Harnett's novel, *Thursday's Child* is a surreal and epic piece of theatre that explores the themes of memory, fate, family camaraderie and the spirit of determination when faced with cruel misfortune.

Teacher's notes are available.

ISBN 978 0 86819 887 3

The Zeal Theatre Collection
Tom Lycos and Stefo Nantsou

Addressing powerful and complex social issues for young people in a safe and respectful manner is at the core of Zeal Theatre's work.

The Stones is based on a true story of two boys charged with manslaughter after throwing rocks from a freeway overpass and killing a motorist. It asks the question whether the boys were old enough to be responsible for their actions.

Burnt is a bush yarn, born and bred out of the true stories of people from regional Australia struggling with prolonged dryness. It looks at the impact of the stresses and strains of continued drought on families and young people.

Taboo is both a warning to young people who might make themselves sexually vulnerable through date rape, and a celebration of a young woman brave enough to tell her story. It looks at the varying degrees of sexual exploitation in the modern age.

'More than anything else Zeal is alive… Zeal are keepers of a flame where theatre is connected directly to its audience, fuelled by their concerns and their questions, charged with their well-being and the quandaries that endanger their very hearts and souls on a daily basis.' Andrew Upton and Cate Blanchett

ISBN 978 0 86819 906 1

pickers stay on the farm and welcomes them into the haven she has created for herself and her teenage daughter, Zoe. Struggling with the burden of living her life within Celia's boundaries, Zoe falls for Kieran and Celia's worst fears are realised when they leave the sanctuary of her farm and disappear.

Told with Oswald's trademark warmth, humour and understanding, *The Peach Season* is a wonderfully moving play about first love and the love between a mother and daughter.

ISBN 978 0 86819 805 7

Skate
Debra Oswald

Inspired by true events, Skate is about a group of kids battling with their local council to get a skate park. When tragedy strikes, the battle grows into a struggle for acceptance and unity.

A turbo-charged, moving and funny account of the mates, mothers, tricks and traumas of a group of young skaters. Enhanced by live skateboarding, the play is full of the emotional awkwardness of adolescence, its adrenalin, compassion and humour.

ISBN 978 0 86819 727 2

Stories in the Dark
Debra Oswald

Winner of the 2008 NSW Premier's Literary Awards

Winner of the 2008 AWGIE Award (Theatre for Young Audiences)

A terrified 12-year-old boy finds himself separated from his family in the unfamiliar streets of a war torn city. He takes refuge in a bombed-out house and in the total blackness his bravado crumbles into tears.

Into his life steps Anna – older, street smart and scornful of his crying. As a way of shutting the boy up, she starts to tell him a story that she vaguely remembers from her own childhood. And so begins a journey into the shifting, shimmering world of ogres, princes, singing bones, foolish lads and wolf-mothers.

Stories in the Dark explores the power of storytelling, mingling the magic and earthy wisdom of folk tales with the hard-edged story of violence, conflict and the struggle to survive.

ISBN 978 0 86819 831 6

www.ingramcontent.com/pod-product-compliance
Lightning Source LLC
Chambersburg PA
CBHW041934090426
42744CB00017B/2057